THE INTERVIEW BLUEPRINT

PROCESS-DRIVEN INTERVIEW SUCCESS: YOUR ROADMAP TO ACHIEVING 2X EARNINGS

RAMENDRA MALTHIYAR

INDIA • SINGAPORE • MALAYSIA

ISBN 979-8-89066-986-5

CONTENTS

ACKNOWLEDGMENT

I acknowledge my father "Sri Vinod Prasad Malthiyar" who has mentored me in the journey of writing books. I am very fortunate to have his support, which has given me many positive thoughts and ideas while writing the manuscript and finishing it appropriately.

His command over the language has helped me to get the book reviewed. It was a great help. I am very thankful to him.

DO YOU KNOW?

- Why do so many people don't clear most of the interview while many of them clear most of it?
- Are you scared of facing an interview?
- Are Corporates becoming more complex in selecting a candidate?
- Is the interview an art or science?
- Does the interview involve some sort of process, or do we just go for an interview on the basis of knowledge that we have?
- Is there anything called a competency-based interview?
- Is dressing sense important?
- Does your body language have any role to play in this process of an interview?
- Is the first impression the last one?
- How one should get acclimatized to the competencies required for the role even if they are not trained in the Organisation or colleges?

Do you have all these questions in mind... WOW ... BINGO ... this book is for you.

CORPORATE COMPLEXITIES VS ASPIRING CANDIDATES

Do you feel that corporates have become more complex? Their lookout for a candidate is like an **"All in One"** kind. Have these corporates become more demanding or the requirements have changed

India has many colleges that offer professional degrees like MBA and Engineering. There are various grades given to the colleges which are based on their teaching methodology and placements status. All these colleges concentrate on teaching their course syllabus and completing them with full dedication, making both teachers and students happy. They later prepare for exams and be happy with the marks while waiting for their placements to take place in their dream companies. Some of them get into their own start-up business or join their family business. Now comes a real-time issue. 'A' grade Colleges' teaching is good and they pay attention to other competency development as well. This is just because their selection process is good along with their placement records. In addition to this, they advertise in the best magazines and papers and gain importance. I agree they have cream students and therefore teaching, and placements are not too difficult. These colleges are very few.

My main concern is B schools and Engineering colleges which fall into the categories of 2nd best grade College as per the ranking of colleges which are in huge numbers across. These colleges and Universities are approx.75% of the total number of colleges. What about their placement? I have taught in some of these colleges and visited a few of them and found that the students are good at studies, and understand subjects well but then what is the issue? This is a big question that keeps me pondering in my head.

A boy from a small town appeared for the management exam. He was through in most of the 'B' school. The boy studied the Vernacular language in his hometown. His written test used to go well but again other parameters like communication and presentation skills were always a stumbling block (not up to mark). Despite his good innate skills, he lacked those powerful competencies which could attract interviewers. In the business world communication is first understood as English language speaking skills and later comes writing. Getting through the interviews or group discussions was an upheaval task. You need to be at least competent in your English communication skills and may not be too fluent. Otherwise the boy is out of the race... very unfortunate!! Corporates get better guys who can communicate and present themselves quite well. This population is no less in the market ...You know!!... no dearth of people in the market!! Why will they bother about the guy who does not have good communication skills as better candidates are available in the market? Now coming to engineering colleges, the scene over here is worrisome. These boys are technically very sound and can do all the work which requires a techy brain, where the least of communication skills are required. They have to solve problems of machines where logic and technical knowledge are required. These guys are required to face interviews to get through and then they can use technical expertise on the job. An interview is the process of selection where communication plays an important role. The process is the same, appearing for an interview where your communication and expression are tested and then a call is taken to hire the person. Practical technical skills are tested later when they join the organization.

Another boy from Bihar (vernacular language speaking belt) got through most of the engineering colleges but could not clear the interview process in many colleges. Finally, he managed to get through in one of the colleges. After becoming an engineering graduate, he appeared for government service exams and cleared most of them with flying colours and now he is an Assistant Deputy Magistrate in one of the government bodies and doing well.

In these two cases who is wrong? The teaching methodology/system or private Corporates. The latter's requirement will not change as these private organizations need those skills to be in the system because of varieties of logical reasons. The government openings are very less in number so all of them will not get hired by such Organisations. You cannot keep blaming the education system and do nothing for them. Since changing the education system is not in our hands, colleges, and universities should take the initiative to do so. How much of it is happening, I am not sure. The full ecosystem is changing. This world has become a knowledge world. We can find knowledge and awareness around every nook & corner. Social media and the internet have created "good evil" in everyone, especially the younger generation. Everyone is glued to smart mobile and listens to so many videos of different types which are readily available. In case they come across a problem in their studies, the immediate guide is "Google Baba". Everyone wants to solve the problem and no one wants to invest time in searching and researching the problem. Therefore, superficial knowledge is gaining ground profusely. But again, it is no one's fault. The access to information and knowledge is so abundantly available in the market that the importance of reading multiple books on a topic nowadays is unheard of. Look at the shift! On the one hand, it is good also in this kind of fast economy we are in, but banking on the internet and not putting effort into reading and exploring can become a stumbling block in the future. Google Baba become quicker now.

Look at the academic results students are getting 99% and 100%. Do they have those required competencies and skill sets to sell themselves in the market is a question to ponder over. Again with so much of the fast-moving world and the existence of the VUCA (volatility, uncertainty, complexity, and ambiguity) world, the prevalence of uncertainties remain and the same shall stay for ages now. You cannot change the education system every now and then. Colleges and universities should add relevant topics or courses as additives to the education system to make it full-fledged. They should provide a wholesome approach. Prepare tea with ginger aroma and do not put sugar. What will be the taste of the tea if you are not diabetic and are not allowed to take sugar in your tea? You may drink it but it is tasteless. I know you will not enjoy it. Therefore, colleges and universities should look into the type of sugar they want to add to the tea. Sugar can be brown, white, or sugar-free as per the choice in order to bring taste to the tea which will give you and your guests a nice feeling and flavour. This is the requirement that all colleges and Universities should imbibe, putting required additives to make it holistic. This initiative by the education institutes will help students to get better placements and better salary deals. Management and Engineering colleges should look into adding sugar to the recipe while ensuring that competencies are becoming better. These students are your ambassadors for the future. Deans and senior management should understand this and start working on this. Help to build a career and not run only colleges. You will get admission but taste tea for God's sake. We cannot change the requirements of the Corporates. The requirements are based on lots of other requirements of theirs, so there is no point in forcing them to change. Rather we should provide the required inputs. Colleges and universities should bring the students to the expectation of the corporates and cannot vice versa. Soft skills and leadership development should be part of their curriculum apart from course studies. I remember the time when I was working in the automobile sector. We wanted a huge number of diploma holders every year. Diploma colleges were identified from where we will pick up candidates. We introduced a small curriculum to fulfil our requirements in the college syllabus. Look what is the result! We started getting ready-made candidates. Our curriculum encompasses technical and soft skills requirements from our own group companies. We have seen results after hiring and putting them to work.

A couple of decades ago Engineering was well sorted out profession. You need to be exceptionally good at getting through in the Engineering college. These lads were highly valued in the society. The scenario in the market started changing. Overseas started demanding engineers from India. More Engineering colleges opened up. Indian Industries were unable to absorb everyone and therefore un-employability started increasing. The Engineering stream started losing glamour. Many of them tried for overseas employment but they do not clear because of a lack of communication and other related soft skills. They might be great in Engineering but clearing interview needs good communication and other soft skills which started becoming a stumbling block. Apart from an outdated curriculum and lack of practical experience, their communication skills were a big challenge. Colleges and Universities do not pay much heed to improving the communication and other soft skills of the students. Students coming from small towns and villages grossly lack communication in English.

Even Indian companies started giving importance to English communication as the first selection criterion. The result was, only smart students with good communication used to get shortlisted. That does not mean that they are technically sound as well. In fact, many of the students who are not very great in English communication are technically very sound and could be a good asset to the organization but lack the main criteria for selection i.e. English communication. The organization has reason to give importance to English communication as the most important selection criterion. They have overseas clients, or their business spread is overseas where English communication plays a very important role. Otherwise, an organization will have one more training area identified from the day the person joins. Hence it is better to get candidates who have those soft skills

Leadership qualities and other soft skills knowledge have always been found the areas of improvement in either "B school or T schools". If you have this required soft skills knowledge, then other skills can be learned. Even soft skills can be learned but these skills take time to grasp and execute. Training on these skills should take place in the initial phase of their college either engineering or management so that by the time they face the interview the knowledge is already there ingrained in them. Colleges and Universities should start thinking along these lines and make them part of their curriculum.

I have seen many good and intelligent students not able to cross the interview and group discussion hurdles because they lack English communication skills and over a period of time they get into a complex cocoon and do not come out. This leads to depression and anxiety and finally breakdown. Colleges and universities are not doing enough to hone these skills in students. You will be surprised that these students clear exams and interviews in their own vernacular language with good marks and ranks. The way the economy is going and ecosystem complexity is increasing while privatization is always on the agenda of the government. You never know when most government organizations turned into private organisation where these soft skills will play a very important role. Candidates having these soft skills will get preference over others. The trend has already got up in the last two decades. In the future, this trend will become perhaps the most important landmark to get through. In case colleges or universities do not start paying heed to this, then they will become responsible for unemployment in the country. On the other hand, the education system needs a complete revamp. These are the two sides of the coin. On the government side of the coin, we cannot do much. But can we not add value to the students through our own understanding of the market for the benefit of the students and so the colleges? Colleges and Universities can introduce soft skills in the curriculum so that the students can take the leaf of faith and get employed. Look at the irony, they start learning these skills in the organization where they join rather in the colleges. They enter into the further complex zone when the peers/juniors start getting attention and better grading in Performance Appraisal. By the time it is late and cannot be retrieved.

There are so many other soft skills apart from English communication that candidates aspiring to get into good organizations need to have. You will find colleges in metro cities have fewer problems than in other cities. They have got some of those required soft skills. These skills are not completely unknown. To my surprise, I have found professors in many colleges lack in these skills then how and what we can expect from the students? I have taken responsibility to highlight and discuss some of the importance of soft skills in students which will give a higher chance of getting better placements. In the process, may I request or recommend colleges or universities to pay attention to these gaps otherwise their institutes will go down in the ranks over the period of time assuming that these institutes are not here to mint money only and do not pay attention to the dire need of the market? Ideally, there should be one subject in the curriculum where students can learn these qualities. They should ideally announce through advertisement that this is one additional course they have in the curriculum. You will find students flocking toward that college or universities will be more. It becomes win -win situation for the institutes.

I will be referring to the set of skills in my discussions and highlighting their benefits to the aspirants. This will not confine only to institutes for getting placement in future.

JOHARI WINDOW

Do you know what you know and others know too? Or do you know what you do not know? You will get to know every bit of you.

Johari Window is developed by Joseph Luft and Harry Ingham. It is a 4-box matrix that looks at what is KNOWN and UNKNOWN in yourself and others. It helps to improve self–awareness and self – communication. It is divided into 4 quadrants

JOHARI MODEL

	Known to self	Not known to self
Known to others	OPEN AREA	BLIND SPOT
Not known to others	HIDDEN AREA	UNKNOWN

- ➤ **The Open Area** (known by yourself, and known by others too)
- ➤ **The Blind Spot** (unknown by yourself, but known by others)
- ➤ **The Hidden Area** (known by yourself, but unknown by others)
- ➤ **The Unknown** (unknown by yourself, and unknown by others too)

JOHARI WINDOW ACTION PLAN

	Known to self	Not known to self
Known to others	DEVELOPMENT DISCUSSIONS	SEEK FEEDBACK
Not known to others	SHARE AREA	FRESH CHALLENGES

TOOLS FOR PERSONAL DEVELOPMENT

The above window talks about personal development and Johari Window provides another complementary and unique perspective. Each window has developmental plans:

1. **OPEN AREA**: Ideal for personal development discussions
2. **THE BLIND SPOT**: Creates an opportunity to seek feedback
3. **HIDDEN AREA**: Gives an opportunity to share thoughtfully
4. **THE UNKNOWN**: Offers you an opportunity to unlock your potential with fresh challenges

Let me elaborate on the following players in defining the Johari window. In this case there are 4 variables acting:

1. Employees
2. University or colleges
3. Advisor or Consultants
4. Students

1. **Open Area** - Employer and future employees are fully aware of the gap that needs to be fulfilled, There are discussions around it. Some employees take their own effort to learn through books or YouTube. Good at least they are trying to do some self-development. Here institutions should play the role. Employers are always upfront in advertisements, pre-placement talks, or JD and the required soft skills competencies for the position. The selections are accordingly done.

2. **Blind Spot** - There are many soft skills competencies required by the prospective employer which students may not be knowing. The institutes know about it. What steps have the institutes taken to bridge the gap and

make students more employable? Institute's role is very crucial in this space. They know the market and understand the various requirements of the market, apart from course materials to enhance employability. Are they doing anything about this? Ask questions like what steps have they taken in this line to improve the competencies of employees? I am sure that this cannot be a blind spot for them.

3. **Hidden areas** - You know yourself the best. All these college students are grown-up lads. They have access to social media and are grown up enough to understand how the job market is behaving and the requirements of the corporates. They also know where they are lacking in terms of soft skills and competencies. There are many competencies required for every student to prosper in their career. These students clearly know which of the two skill sets that they need hand-holding or training for their development. They are sharing that with others or not is a different thing. You know your areas of improvement since you know yourself the best. Here comes the institute's role, they know the market dynamics and requirements. They can make a small bouquet of training and development for students and train them in those skills. While other areas of development, students can take ownership of themselves and develop. These are the attributes expected from Institutes and students, or else they will enter into an unknown zone which is devastating or "hara-kiri" for that matter. The career of the students will be completely spoilt and who knows even institutes will have their doom days coming. Neither institute nor the students cut corners in the areas of development. Avoid getting into the unknown zone indicated in the Johari window.

4. **The unknown** - This is a fun zone that is dangerous at the same time. It is the situation where most of the institutes and students are today. This should not be taken as negative. This is the most challenging zone where consultants are required to show the path and help both institute and students to carve a better path of soft skills training and development for the good of both the parties- students and institution /community. Consider this as a challenging time and head towards developing it. Once the grey area is known then development will take place. I am sure this dump box is known to everyone, and they are working towards it for a better future. Everyone has to come to the forefront and take these challenges up front as the ecosystem is changing very fast and we need to

pull up our socks and sail on the boat, otherwise, no one will stop both to get capsized. Yes, all of us are moving in the right direction to tide over these challenges.

The Johari window is meant for discussion and self-development. I have given a different perspective with the same meaning. Let us become a torch bearers and help both parties to attend the same milestone and goals.

Good personality and character

I remember when I was in college, there was a very handsome tall guy who used to come to the college on a bullet motorcycle. He had all the required attractions required to impress any opposite sex. He came from a rich family, and coming on a bullet in those days was itself an attraction since no one had at that time. His personality was talked about in college, especially among girls. We were of course very jealous of him. While we were starving for one relationship with the girl of our choice. He had girls flocking around him. You will find him sitting with one in the morning and the second one in the evening. It is obvious that we will feel a bit jealous just because we were in a drought and he was enjoying Cherapunji with girls. He could easily and strategically get along with girls. Everybody in the college admires his personality to be the best. Is it a personality or character that we have been judging him for? You know whatever we have been discussing so far is a very miniscule part of his personality. I agree he was good-looking and smart. But what has he done for his good-looking and smart look? he has done nothing at all. It is a mere accident of two people and he is the product of that. He is taking advantage of something for which he has not done anything. Look at the external side of him. The bullet that he brought was purchased by his father. Therefore he has nothing of him but look at the irony of everyone talking of his personality. Let me combine personality and character together. The personality of a person is built by the character he has. The character is not built with the looks and bike that he has kept. It is built by many characteristics to name a few as follows:

1. Integrity
2. Honesty
3. loyalty.
4. Compassion.
5. Politeness.
6. Kindness
7. Self-Discipline
8. Humility
9. Courageous
10. Reliability
11. Perseverance

Now are these traits being taught in the colleges? If you go and ask someone what is the meaning of personality, students will refer to the ones I have stated as per my experience in college.

Let me define the two:
Personality can be defined as a combination of mental behaviour and thinking patterns of an individual to think, feel and behave in a specific manner in diverse situations. It refers to systematic dispositions like attitude thoughts and feelings/ emotions. In addition to it if you have a good physical personality then it becomes an added advantage to your personality.

But this can never be the sole definition of personality whereas character means enduring and distinguishing mental and moral characteristics in an individual. It is the factor that determines our response to a given event or situation. It defines the person's behavior pattern and thinking style. It depends on the kind of environment that one stays. Let me differentiate between personality and character for a better understanding.

Though the difference between the two is not very easy to explain and most of the time they intermingle with each other. Have those understandings been clear to you otherwise, you will remain captivated with the understanding of personality with an external physical look while a character with non-involvement in any unethical activities. The students should understand to differentiate between the two and inculcate good features of both.

You can easily correlate with the below-tabulated details which will help to understand this in a better way. Perhaps this would be useful in the future to distinguish a bleak line between the two

Sr. No	PERSONALITY	CHARACTER
1	Combination of qualities, attitudes, and behavior that makes a person different	Set of moral and mental beliefs that makes a person different from others
2	Set of personal Qualities. It implies who we seem to be	Set of mental and moral characteristics. Represents who we are! !
3	Person's identity	Are learned/ acquired behavior
4	Subjective	Objective
5	Outer appearance or behavior of the person	Indicates hidden traits of the person
6.	Personality may change with time	Character lasts long
7	Do not need validation or support of society	Requires validation and support of the society

Therefore, Personality can be termed as the outer wall whereas characteristics are an inner wall.

If a college girl moves around with different boys who are her friends unless she declares one as her boyfriend. Here look at the perception being created. The first thing that comes to mind with most of the male counterparts is that the girl is" characterless". What does that mean? Is it because she moves around with different guys? Believes in parting out or she spends the night out with a group of boys and girls. What does the word "characterless "mean? The term is very loosely said over here just because of the lack of actual meaning of the term. Then that becomes their vocabulary forever.

Johari windows box should not be the case of students who are not aware of these valid characteristics while others are aware of them. They are always on the scanner from the actual understanding point of view which will be very useful once they enter the corporate world.

This is what I have been mentioning the basic understanding which could make them a better professionals. The institution should ensure that these things should become part of the curriculum or take help from external experts to make this ongoing learning to the students towards building a better profession once they enter the corporate world. The clarity of these nuances should be from the very beginning. The bringing up should be towards developing leaders and not only making them good professionals though both jargons are more or less same. But creating perception and working towards building leaders and not only professionals should be the goal.

Chetan Bhagat's book half girlfriend mentions a boy from Bihar who came to Delhi and got into college through sports quota (basketball). He came across a very rich girl from a business family in Delhi. Both came very close and started spending time together. The girl was from a very rich industrialist family. Her many relatives were staying abroad. The family can never think of getting their daughter married to such a lower-class person. The girl was at a marriage age and the family was looking for a boy of the same status. Engaging a boy from overseas was also one of the thoughts in the family. They want someone of that stature for their daughter, which was neither wrong nor difficult to get. The girl was also very clear that this boy from Bihar cannot be approved by her parents as a life partner. So, she was careful in dealing with him. The boy has started loving her, though she was also attracted but being from Delhi and a rich family, she was able to control her feeling. She liked him because of his character. His down-to-earth attitude, honest behaviour no show-off, openness, and conscientious nature were the qualities that attracted the girl. But then she knew he was not meant for her because of her family background and stature in society. The guy was tall smart and good-looking but did not appeal because of the family stature. It was his good nature, character, and personality that appealed to her. Most of us know the story and if it is Mr. Chetan Bhagat's book it will have spice into it.

LEADERSHIP DEVELOPMENT

"If your actions inspire others to dream more, learn more, do more, and become more, you are a leader." You are a leader, plug some gaps and that's it …

Once you join any organization, within a couple of months you start hearing leadership jargon too often. Then you start pondering what does it really mean? When you were in college you read the role of a manager which is planning coordinating, directing and organizing etc. You have been taught these things in your college and you immediately start connecting with them. You have also read something about leadership. As a student, you are unable to differentiate between the two i.e. leader and manager. Now who is going to put unnecessary pressure on the brain? You clear all your exams and be happy with the marks and wait for the placement to happen. I do understand that it is none of your fault. I remember when I had been to one of the management colleges to conduct a session and asked the question about the qualities of leadership. Most of the students talked about the manager's role which they have read in their college. Though I understand at such young age this question would be a bit taxing. But things are moving at a very fast pace. Institutes must buck up and catch the fast pace and make the study readymade to be sold in the market. We were doing the same things in our college days. We were reading one or two books only which help us to fetch good marks. We all were happy including our parents as every things were going smoothly. There was no specific guidance given to us apart from scoring good marks, which we were doing. Our thoughts were very limited as there was no proper guidance as to how to build a career. I, as an HR practitioner, thought of intervening and sharing these concepts with management and engineering students in their respective institutes and making them aware of the requirements outside their campus. You may like to refer to my book**." Leaders do not only talk but**

Walk the Talk "Amazon's #1 best seller. This book is more towards different leadership styles, but you all can understand the qualities and traits required in a good leader. Let me give you some practical "Gyan" (knowledge) about the leadership qualities or traits which we should acquire and learn if we are not born with them. Some of the important leadership qualities you also know and imbibe in you going forward and not succumbing to any pressure.

1. **Walk the talk:** It is very simple to do what you say and say what you do. This means you should be very careful when you speak anything even when you casually say so. Till the time you are junior, you can still sail through but when you become senior every word that you speak have meaning and people take it at face value. If you do not stick to what you say you are on the wrong radar. Though people won't say anything you are "whispered" in the town. Be very cautious about it.

I remember the story told by Mr. Rahul Bajaj – MD of Bajaj Auto, a very humble and down-to-earth personality. No air on his nose because of his position. He stated that once a very rich man met his great-grandfather when he was a small boy and was impressed. The rich man said that he would like to take that kid home as he liked him very much. Great grandfather's mother in Rajasthani style told that the boy is his, and he can take him. All these conversations were very casually done. Now the rich man said that he would take his grandfather (young boy then) home which was very surprising to the mother of the grandfather, since she thought all the while the discussions/talk was just normal. The father of Rahul Bajaj's grandfather told his wife when they have agreed to something even if that was acausal talk, they should honor their word, otherwise, it would be a wrong example set and the family. This is how the young boy was taken by the rich man and the rest of his history. Rahul Bajaj said that he was lucky that the person was his great-grandfather and hence he amass so much wealth and prosperity. I the grandfather of his security guard was taken in the rich family then Rahul Bajaj would be the security guard and the latter would be the former. He wanted to mention more on circumstances than walk the talk. But I thought of stating it as this would serve both purposes. The example may not be too apt but still thought of quoting it to explain the leadership side of Rahul Bajaj, a very young Industrialist.(Excerpts from Rahul Bajaj's interview. A very inspiring and practical)

Understanding some of the meanings and explanations of leadership qualities by college students would keep them connected quickly when they are in the corporate world. It would also help them to inculcate those qualities at an early age.

2. **Communication skills**: This skill is perhaps our most important competency in all these aspiring students. I will not explain what communication is as I am sure everyone is aware of it. The communication process is speak – decode – encode. All of you know the barriers to communication try and overcome those to make communication smooth. The result is that your message should be understood by others so that action can be taken. The most important is your language and that to the English language. Whether one likes it or not the English language is a very important medium of communication in India, despite our commonly spoken language being Hindi. There are a lot of advantages to knowing the English language and making it a part of communication. All interviews are conducted in English language which becomes difficult for candidates who are not minimum and reasonably conversant with the language. It becomes a barrier for him. Therefore, improve upon your weakness and be ready for the requirement. It is not very hard to learn this competency. You just need reasonable English communication to cross through an interview in the first place and then it will be further useful while working in the office also. You are expected to communicate, and reply to all e-mails in English. Later this competency will help you to excel in other places in the organization. One should develop and improve this quality while studying in college. Why don't you improve when you know this will become an impediment to your growth in the future? This is also one of the qualities of a leader that you know your area of improvement and you are working towards it.

3. **Problem-solving:** This is one of the key skillsets employers seek from budding job seekers, though I understand problem-solving can be learned on the job only, but the knowledge to tackle any problem should be known to newcomers. How does an employee look for a solution to any of the problems?
There are three ways of addressing any problem, especially by people.
Run away or procrastinate.

Involve so many people in it that the problem becomes complex. Instead, brainstorm it in the quality circle forums using a fishbone diagram and solve any problems

Understand the root cause and solve the problems. This means taking ownership and not shirking away because of complexities.

Problem solvers are required by an employer. Raising problems is very easy but solving needs your cognitive brain and responsibilities. Guys who can solve problems and not pass them on to others are sort for by any employer. In case you end up in some complex issue, ask for help but do not buzz off.

I was a trainee in one of the very well-known Birla organizations, which was a manufacturing setup. I found the overtime of the employees was too high. Some workers were earning more than 50% of their salary from overtime. It was a big loss to the company and labour laws were also breached. I took one-year data for each employee and discussed the same with my time office guys. I took out high overtime workers and also discuss case-wise. The outcome of the discussion, I took it up with the line manager. After that, I discussed with the respective heads of the function with my idea. They liked my idea. I reduce over time by 25% and 3 months of time followed by 50% in one year's time by doing the following:

1. Overtime must be divided among all and not only to a few
2. Overtime must be signed and approved by the Head of the Departments.
3. Anyone reaching a particular figure mark needed to be flagged to HOD's and HR head.
4. Proforma was created and the reasons for overtime is to be mentioned.
5. Fortnightly MIS reports on this was generated and shared with Head of the department and Unit Head

At that young age I was handsomely rewarded.

What I did here, all of you can do? Go to basics and ask "why" as per Toyota style. It is the "5 why" method. Ask five times why and you get an answer. The smart way of solving it. A simple way of solving any problem which employees expects are –

➤ Agree there is a problem and the person has to solve and not pass it on.
➤ Take responsibility to solve the problem. Once the above two parameters are accepted by anyone half of the problem is solved. This means someone has taken responsibility to solve the problem.

➤ Go to the root cause of the problem. All is in mind, as I am referring to "day to day" problems to be solved and move on.

➤ What could be the probable solutions to solve them then choose the best one?

4. **Ask for help or report with your solution to the boss:** You should always go with some solutions to any problem to your superiors. They will appreciate it. There are many problems that come up in the cohort. Need problem solvers.

5. **Keep your temperament cool and do not blame anyone:** This attitude is Brahma Shastra. Keep things simple and clear. Your thought process will flow seamlessly and there you hit the bull's eye.

6. **Integrity and ethics:** These qualities depend a lot on the family bringing up. The ethics existing in the family and the same gets manifested in the College /university environment make culture. In this kind of environment, these two values/qualities flourish. We understand these qualities are the backbone of a good human being. It takes a long way. Universities and colleges must inculcate and reinforce these qualities in students in a structured way. These qualities help them to build their career in the future. This also gives a very positive name to the university. These students, no matter how much experience they carry, the tag name of the colleges is always on their backs. These students play a very important role in building culture. They already have those qualities and a deep understanding of them. They can easily connect with the culture and display them very vividly.

Many organizations have their code of conduct where these qualities are discussed with some examples to make the conceptual understanding correct. Ethics are the values that you have of which you feel proud while integrity is again a value system that one possesses that help them to refrain from any unethical practices. You get various opportunities to be unethical and still work with pride. My discussion will look more like "Gyan" (sermon) which is true but the topic is to give "Gyan" only. Let me end this by saying these two qualities are very important to a good professional. Not only that this is also very important for your life lesson. This is life culture. Even if your performance is a bit low but integrity and ethics have no room for negotiations. It is like "zero tolerance".

7. **Teamwork**: Hey guys, future leaders all of you play games like football volleyball or cricket. You must have witnessed many team sports. These sports are team sports. In case any one of the members is a spoilt brat then you succumb before reaching the goalpost. All of you should take each one's responsibility to progress. In case someone is weak help him to cope up so that team remains strong. Recently Commonwealth Games was held in Birmingham. India was playing a hockey match against England. India was leading 3 – 1. Then suddenly two players did fowl and they were made to sit outside for a couple of minutes as per hockey rule. That was the time England conceded two goals and got to equal the goal tally. Otherwise, India was leading and ended in a draw. Can you guess what happened? In a team especially in sports, all the areas are demarcated basis of the strength, and an individual is placed there who is having those strengths/skills. If anyone is missing, the others must take responsibility but the strength of the team weakens. In the case of the hockey match of the Commonwealth Games, there was a huge gap and the team combination faltered in the absence of 2 specialists. Here England could take benefit out of it and score two goals. No you all will understand hoiw important is the team work. It is said united we stand divided we fall which is very true. Though colleges and universities conduct group activities and give emphasis on teamwork. My daughter is studying at an engineering college. She had many group activities. She led in many of the team performances. If the same practical learning is clubbed with classroom training from the same external consultant, the amalgamation of the two activities in team building can give a much better understanding. It will further become gospel when the same is linked to the corporate world which they would enter in a year or so. All these efforts should be taken focusing on the future of the students. The students start thinking very positively and refrain from unnecessary gossiping, and playing politics while developing team spirit. They will slowly start understanding empathy and stakeholder management. Teamwork always takes you miles and every success rejoices the fruit of success.

8. **Stakeholders management:** This is another good recipe that all management and technical graduates should understand and try to inculcate in themselves. These guys are very soon going to enter the

corporate world where they have to manage them through their skills. Your 360-degree management one has to do in the corporate world. If there is a bit of clear understanding from the college itself then they would be able to handle it better once they start working. In the college, you need to understand who the stakeholders across the institutions are. Management of stakeholders means developing governance within yourself. Develop a networking attitude without demeaning or derogating anyone even if the person is your junior. Bear in mind all the stakeholders are important for one's growth therefore consider them as an important partner for your growth. Who are the stakeholders in your college? Your professors, Dean, Registrar, Admin Heads, friends and Colleagues, Hostel management, and some more. Can you survive by making any of these stakeholders unhappy? I do not mean you should become sycophants but be a true professional while dealing with them. Do not undermine their authority and put yourself in trouble. But that does not mean you need to bow down and listen to everything from them like a holy cow. You need to raise your point as appropriate. Ready to take feedback from them and implement. These practices will make you get into the corporate culture. They will identify the stakeholders soon. There is a slight difference between college stakeholders and corporate stakeholders. The former type is dealing with most of the authorities who take a short, whereas corporate world stakeholders a slightly more inequality as all were employees at various levels. Take all the feedback properly.

Friends, I am writing these things from my experience. When I was in my management college and then entered the corporate world, I stumbled in many places because of a lack of understanding of the required skill sets. I have visited a couple of colleges both engineering and management either for some meetings or to deliver some sessions. I have found all these aspiring students have a similar kind of mindset and skill set where I feel the same kind of intervention is required to hone their skills so that they sail through the ever-changing corporate work efficiency, if not too effective in the initial phase. No one is ready to wait. My advice to the institutions is to train the students on these aspects to stand for better employability.

INFLUENCING SKILLS

"There is no better way to influence children than being their role model."
– Eraldo Banovac

Do not think … all of us need this competency to succeed

The skill is very important for any fresher or for that matter anyone who has a positive bent of mind. Influencing skills help to get through in many situations. Influencing comes from your knowledge, skills, and presence of mind. Here skills mean communication and listening skills. Try and understand the question first and do not just jump to answer immediately. Give it a pause, assimilate your thoughts, and then allow an informed answer. Look at the disaster when you do not listen to any questions. This happened to me in one of the interviews. The interviewer started asking a question …" tell me some incident when you persuaded your boss for something............." I jumped in between assuming that the question was finished and answered. The interviewer heard me and then said hold on. "I am yet to complete the question". He added "and the boss did not agree". Actually, I had the answer prefixed in my mind which I answered. Now I cannot add saying that the boss did not agree. There I was under pressure. In this kind of situation, you will find it difficult to regain back your confidence, and then all your skills go for a toss. Therefore, try and jot down some relevant questions and do some practice. Develop good listening skills. Interviewing skills is a very positive connotation and have lots of value. Here your confidence and quality of mind are tested along with communication. Further in addition your skill of taking the team together also comes to light. Do not bother you may fail sometimes. Keep the intent positive and your influencing skills will ooze out in a good way. Let me just give you some examples to lead your thought process. The questions will be more situation based which calls for positive persuasive skills, without any wrong intent in mind. Do not connect these positive skills with politicians' persuasive skills, who are capable enough to show their persuasive and influencing skills even with their wrong intent. Therefore, in this case have a positive frame of mind and look forward with the same eyesight. Influencing skills includes the ability to…

- Clearly communicate your ideas with conviction and logic.
- Active listening skills
- Being calm and assertive
- Situation-based communication
- While you speak, build meaningful relations, and connect with the person
- Throw light on others' needs also while answering any influencing skill questions
- Negotiation skills: Here also your assertiveness and positivity come in play which is a positive sign of your intent.

This also means that you should agree to disagree with someone's viewpoint by listening carefully. You cannot just ignore it since the other person thought process may not match yours. You never knew the other person's views might influence you for some time. The other person on the team also appreciates your dealing. This is also one way of relationship building for the future. This will help that discussion to go smoothly which is another form of influencing tactics.

Therefore this is about behaving in ways that offer others the invitation to change and accommodate your own wishes while accepting others' viewpoints as well.

Robert Cialdini 's principal of influence:

- Commitment: People require consistency.
- Social proof: People do what they observe others doing.
- Authority: People trust authority
- Liking: People prefer similarities
- Scarcity: Fewer quality equals more demand.
- Unity: Us and then.

I am leaving you all to assimilate your thought on the basis of Cialdin's principles. Every word has an in-depth meaning. You should be knowing this though you guys are too young, but gaining knowledge is like having a new soul. Before I end this topic allow me to give you some questions which can be asked to ascertain you in these skills:-

a) Tell about a time when you had a disagreement with the team how have you handled it?

b) Tell me about a time when you had to work with difficult people?

There could be situational questions like this where your influencing skills are tested. My dear readers, there is no right and wrong answer to these questions. The interviews do not check your success rate but they check your approach to handling the situation. How have you put forth your valid and genuine points to influence others? What was your convection while doing so?

Your quality of mind, authority, intent, and conviction are noticed. How did you address the situation? Therefore, do not get misguided that you must always win the situation. You can win the situation by being argumentative, pushing people down, ignoring some valid points to prove yours, and many other so-called unethical ways, just to prove your points. But believe me, this is not influencing skills, this could be called something else. Therefore, analysis of the situation is also very important before you try to influence. It is a very good skill that interviewers will look for in a candidate.

DESIGN THINKING

"We spend a lot of time designing the bridge, but not enough time thinking about the people who are crossing it."

**– Dr. Prabjot Singh,
Director of Systems Design at the Earth Institute**

Design thinking is the process of solving problems by prioritizing the requirement through a systematic process. It draws on logic imagination, intuition, and systematic reasoning to explore the possibilities of what could be and to create desired outcome and benefit for the customer. Though this is very widely used in solving problems in the organization. But all of you should have knowledge that will give you an edge over others. This is the most important and proven process being followed to solve any issues. Many universities and colleges are following this and keep advertising about it. They just want to say that they are either ahead of time or with time by gaining the latest knowledge and implementing it at the same time. Once you know about this topic, I am sure you will start using it at various places in your life and get the desired output. Let me make you all aware of the process with some explanation otherwise this topic can go on and on. There are 5 steps and this process

1. **Empathize** - Gather the need and requirements of the customer. Involved them without if you know everything. Gather the requirements of the target customer. The first step to success. This means you are identifying the problem basis the customer's voice. You are connecting at an emotional and psychological level.

2. **Define** - A prototype is built based on the knowledge that you have amassed by your customer. This needs some discussions amongst the team and a prototype is prepared which can be considered a bit raw unless it is tested and tried. Here this becomes a problem statement.

3. **Ideate** - This is the time to be creative. Here you begin generating ideas for innovative solutions. No idea is a bad idea. Create and decide on an idea to go ahead. You brainstorm and discuss and narrow down to a solution.

4. **Prototype** - Now your idea is done into a tangible product, a rough model, or sketch. The prototype is a scaled-down version of your product. The user may accept or reject.

5. **Test** - This is where you test your solution. Invite users to test and respond to your prototype. The test response will make you understand to take it forward.

Make a model in the book (from google)

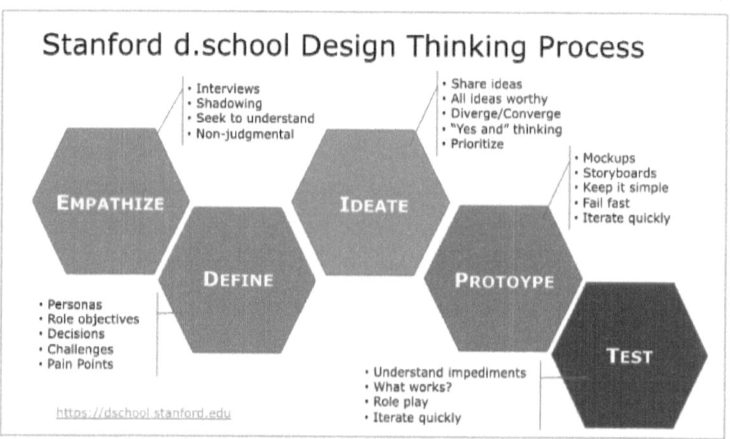

Therefore, design thinking is both ideology and a process concerned with solving complex problems in a highly user-centric way. It focuses on humans first, seeking to understand people's needs and come up with effective solutions to meet those needs. It is based on methods and processes to reach the outcome. It is tried, tested and logical process to arrive at the solution to any complex situation and the same is happily accepted by all. The best part is since it is a process and therefore a team is involved, hence everyone gets the credit.

COMPETENCY DEVELOPMENT

"Competence means keeping your head in a crisis, sticking with a task even when it seems hopeless, and improvising good solutions to tough problems when every second counts. It encompasses ingenuity, determination, and being prepared for anything."

– Chris Hadfield

What is competency? What are the basic competencies which any corporate world like to see in an aspiring student? I am sure the management students are aware of this as this must be part of the course curriculum. Engineering students should also know this which help them once they get into the corporate world. Competency-based interview questions?

Competency interview questions are designed to access whether you have the necessary skills and qualities to carry out the role, you are being interviewed for. Common Competencies

- Team working
- Working under pressure
- Customer service – internal and external
- Problem-solving
- Leadership and management
- Initiative takers

Competency-based questions are to test how you react to a particular question - It is SAR - situation action and result. For example, tell me the time when you complete the target despite so much pressure. Have you ever been in a situation where you disagree with your boss? All these questions should have evidence-based answers.

S - Describe the **situation** you were in

T - **Task** that needed to do

A - Detailed **action** you took

R - Describe the **result** of your action

While answering these questions be very positive. Never criticize anyone or your former employer. Focus purely on what your worth is and how you contribute to the situation.

What is competency?

Competency Model (from Google)

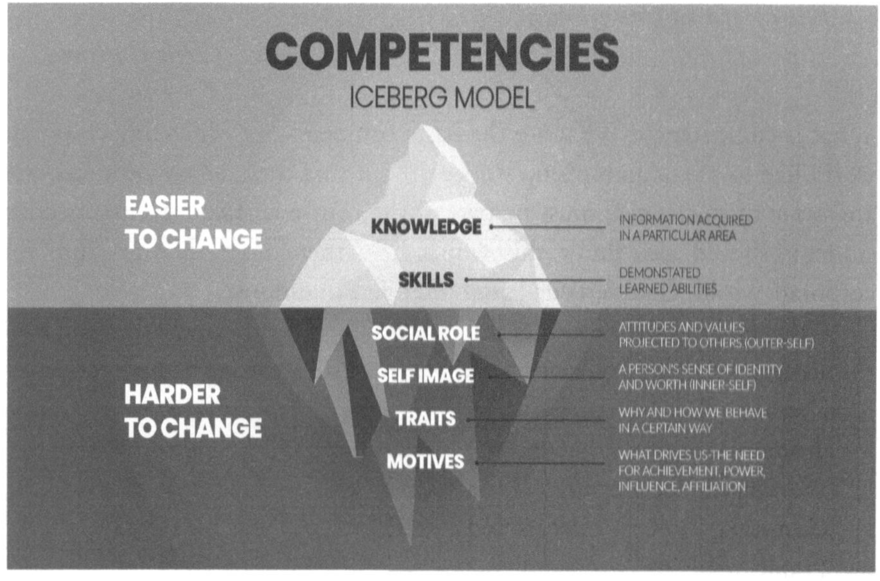

Knowledge - Education and experience along with content knowledge

Skills - Ability to do something well, for example, technical skills.

Self-image - How people see/view themselves the person's worth. Eg. expert leader, change agent, learner, etc.

Traits - Habitual enduring characteristic. Eg. Self-control. good listening skills, engagement, inspiration, and building trust, etc.

In other words, it is SKA skill knowledge and attitude which are demonstrated constantly is competencies.

KASH - knowledge attitude and skills demonstrated habitually.

The competencies below in the iceberg are the drivers to influence the competencies above to deliver better. The influencing factors are below the iceberg which is not seen but can be expressed through knowledge and skills. Even if you have knowledge and skills but no attitude then the result may not be seen. It is said that if your attributes below the iceberg are correct then skills and knowledge can be learned and obtained but vice versa is difficult.

Therefore, there are two types of competencies.
1. Technical Competencies - knowledge and skills required to do the job in the role.
2. Behavioural competencies-traits and characteristics required to do the jobs.

Both are important and complement each other but behavioral competencies add cherry to the cake and make it tasty to have.

SUCCESS

"Success is Not Final, Failure is Not Fatal: it is the Courage to Continue that Counts"

– Winston Churchill

Success is a small improvement every day or at a regular frequency leading to a bigger successful stop. This means constant and consistent change every day in whatever you do. Success is making a decision by being ambitious, listen to your gut.

Earl Nightingale: Success is a progressive realization of a worthy goal or ideal.

Dan Lok (Author, business trainer, and motivational speaker)-Success is a pre-determined plan and successfully executing the plan over a long period of time and having fun doing it.

People get swayed by the money, car, and big house a person possesses success. Let me give you an example. My friend is a filthy rich CEO of a company enjoying everything that money can give but his family life is horrible. The kids do not want to talk, the wife does not stay with him and they hardly meet. Is that a success? In fact, that is a failure in my eyes. Success is not the destination but the quality of your journey. Success is very less to do with money but it has a money component involved too. Let me give you a gross definition of successful. It has a big Canvas and should not look only through the lens of money. In fact, money will automatically get attracted when one starts becoming successful. My definition is like something more and deeper where I need to find out answers of the following: -

1. Am I impacting other people's life and contributing to society?
2. Am I contributing to the happiness of the family?
3. How do I feel about myself when I look in the mirror?

4.   Humility is a great sign of success.
5.   Targeting something and working consistently towards achieving it.
6.   Do some improvement every day. Get up in the morning and plan what new things you want to do. Rise every day with small steps.
7.   Make some life goals and work towards them.
8.   Do not keep a lot of expectations from others. Like you give a party and expect others to give. Why did you give the party then in the first place?
9.   It has a deeper and long tunnel.
10. It should give motivation and a positive kick every day.
11. Say that you and be selfless in any relationship
12. Do not forget your old friends or just go a long mile to help your friends and anyone whom you care.
13. Social status.
14. Always associate with positive-minded people (quality people).

Therefore, success is the mindset that controls our thoughts you need to nurture your mind. Our thoughts become actions and actions produce outcomes. Your success is to begin living by your own terms and conditions. This starts by focusing your actions on activities that bring you joy, a sense of fulfillment, and service to others in defining true success for yourself. You need to stay true to a more profound sense of purpose and meaning. You need to have the courage to pursue your own journey when confronted by the fear, and uncertainty that life will throw at us. You need to choose your own path, you need to be conscious about living to your core values that genuinely allow you to connect to a cause or community that goes beyond yourself. Whatever success you achieve should positively impact others' lives.

In other words, success is very simple to do things that make you happy. My way of looking at success is helping others. I contribute a lot in an old age home and blind schools and many times to keto. When I do this, you do not know how satisfied I sleep. I cannot see the misery and pain of others. Of course, I have my own limitations to do so. Every year I donate blankets to needy people. Once I was doing at night one girl came and told me that instead of a blanket can I give her milk so that her small brother can drink it and they can prepare tea also for the family. Since I was not carrying that I told her to wait for some time and I will get it for her. At night I went around the market bought those articles and gave them to her. The young girl said that she was sure I will not come back and was surprised to see I came back as no one comes back. This brings another point to talk on the subject of success. Keep promises whether it is for a poor man or a very rich influential man. By keeping a promise do you think you make the other person happy, it is a big "no." you are making yourself happy. Let me give you another dimension, people tend to keep promises more for those influential men in order to get some benefits from them. Selfish motive. If you keep promises of some poor people who cannot give any benefits in return but the number of unheard blessings that you get cannot be measured. The bottom line is that I adhere to this whether it is spoken casually or on a serious note. In case I do not adhere to my words which I thought I would, I clarify with the person and put an end to the topic. This makes me happy though there is no extrinsic gain but intrinsic for sure.

Success is important for everyone. One can define the same in their own language and be consistent. The bottom line is that whatever makes you happy and keeps you healthy do it but try and give a broader outlook and make success more sustainable.

Though I know in the initial phase of life you need to work to earn for yourself but later you may like to curb the flywheel a bit and work for others (society). India is a very big country and needs voluntary contribution from everyone in one's own way. I am just trying to provide a broad explanation of success for your consumption and understanding.

FEEDBACK

"We all need people who will give us feedback. That's how we improve."
– Bill Gates

Feedback is a powerful development lever in the workplace. It helps people to understand their strengths, weaknesses, and how others perceive them - so that they can become the best version of themselves.

This is very important, especially for students. One who takes the positive frame of mine prospers while others get caught into more complications. All of you are mature with a smart head over your shoulder and you easily understand who genuinely gives feedback and who flatters. When you wish to take feedback go to your well-wisher. When your well-wisher gives negative feedback take it positively and work on the same. There are many people who do not like hearing negative feedback and then look at what happens in a story. It goes like this.

A bird requested a tree to make a nest on top. She said monsoon is coming before that she would like to make a nest so that its children will stay comfortable in the rainy season. The trees said "no" it won't allow the bird to make a nest. The bird was very angry and went to another tree with the same request. The second agreed and allowed her to make a nest. The bird make the nest and started living. Rainy season came. Lots of rain fell. The place was filled with water. The first tree which did not allow the bird to make a nest got uprooted and started flowing with the water flow. The bird was very happy and said good "You are drowning as you did not help when I requested for. It wanted to say since the tree did not let it make a nest on trees and that is the reason god has punished the tree. The tree said that it did not allow it because it knew that its root is weak, anytime it can be uprooted. The bird's nest would also fall down and children will die. The bird realized and felt sorry about the first tree.

The lesson is that all negative or no answer does not mean bad or something that you feel bad about and start cursing the person. Remember the moment one door closes, there are many doors open. This means that there are other opportunities waiting to get grabbed. Therefore, feedback of any form negative or positive should always be looked at with a positive lens and take a call appropriately. One of the greatest poets of India Kabir Das has said that people who give negative feedback to you on the face are your best well-wisher, at least you take it positively and keep improving upon it. Do not let the positive feedback set on your head and the negative devastate you. Take it on merit and take negative feedback as God's sent while considering this as an area of improvement and working towards it.

Giving and receiving feedback is an art. Organizations encourage this a lot. They provide training to this account so that feedback in any form should be acceptable in the right spirit. Feedback given in an act of vengeance is not correct, do not underestimate the receiver, he immediately understands it and acts accordingly. Feedback is the best form of communication that encourages improvements and organizations want it to institutionalize it for the good of the organizations. Feedback with the right intentions can bring wonders. I have seen cases where communication is not properly addressed or people are not ready to accept negative feedback is a very sad state of affairs. I have witnessed that even in a 360-degree feedback process, people are unwilling to give negative feedback properly. They use very vulgar ways of addressing which is wrong. People do not accept negative feedback in a derogatory way. The feedback is given in such a way that means you cannot speak so badly on the face you choose to pen. In fact that talks mean-mindedness about the guy who has given negative feedback with derogatory words. The feedback process still needs to institutionalize and considers as an improvement radar. The Giver and receiver of the feedback are equally responsible to communicate in the right way while following the decorum. Most of the time negative feedback takes the front seat based on one incident and especially when it has taken place recently.

Gentlemen, this is a very important tool for progression, so take it in the right spirit. Sometimes you may take it as a pinch of salt but take it and work on the improvement. The best thing about the feedback of both types is known by the person in question. There are very few blind spots that one is not aware of. Otherwise, one knows about himself quite well. Wise people take positive feedback properly without putting air on the nose while negative feedback takes it as an area of improvement and works towards it. As I said let me repeat people who give feedback derogatorily are also understood by the receiver and take it as per merit. No one is a fool, my dear. Therefore, my final submission of giving and receiving constructive feedback is part and partial of your life. Remember Kabir Das, who said the best way to improve is to keep someone who gives negative feedback very close. So that you improve every day and every moment. Let me repeat again all of us know our strengths and weaknesses therefore we can easily understand who is flattering and who is genuine. Just look at the feedback process, which is the way to improve. Hope you all are with me so far.

Let me personally write my message to the youngsters for whom I am writing this book. Take feedback in any form either in person or through the third person. Analyze with an open mind and act on it. The tendency is that all good feedback is acceptable and negative feedback is considered "they are not for me". It can also connotes that the other person is jealous of him therefore he is giving the wrong feedback. No way, if there is more than one person giving the same feedback, "O boy" you need to soul search and improve upon to become a better person and personality going forward. Just remember Kabir Das.

SELF-DEVELOPMENT

"Learn to work harder on yourself than on your job."

– Jim Rohn

Dear students, allow some time from your busy schedule of attending classes, enjoying at the canteen, pulling each other legs, going trekking, trying to get a girlfriend, or freaking out with girls for self-development.

When I was in my graduation college days, I was a bit fat compared to others. Trying to showcase my development. Please do not get confused by the word self-development by developing yourself only from the point of study. Whatever you do for yourself is self-development. Let me tell you, my story. Since I was back, I thought of shedding my weight and then running was the only way. I am not a sportsman and I will look very odd on the ground when so many sportsmen or fit people doing their morning raga. But I stored all my guts and convinced myself that I should start running sooner than later. You know how did I convince myself!!!! Once I went to the football ground in Pune where I was studying, I sat there for an hour and saw everyone walking, jogging, or doing specific sports-related exercises. I was happy to find that there was no one on the ground to whom I know. That gave me the motivation to get on the ground in the morning. I overcame one challenge. The second challenge, (which was more often an excuse) I did not have proper track pants. Do you know what happened? My friend's brother had just returned from the USA, he gave me a gift of track pants. Now I was left with no excuse. Now I have all the resources with me to start my jogging. I took the decision that I will start my job the very next day. Getting up early in the morning was never a problem for me. The next day onwards I started running. And you know what! In 3 to 4 months' time, I started running 22 rounds of the football ground which was the maximum. There were some girls who also used to come and jog for 10 to 12 rounds which at that young age motivated me to go for more. At that young age, those thoughts are very common. Who will know better than you guys (college students). In the next 6 months of time, I reduce 12 kgs. From that time onwards till today, I get up very early and do some jogging almost 4 to 5 days a week. Further to add to this I have participated in 15 half marathons and long-running events of. 10-15 km events, I must have participated more than 20 times in this long-running event.

I have cited my example just to motivate you guys to spare some time for self-development which is very important as it stays with you for a lifetime. Another way of doing self-development is to just put yourself in, and start improving by looking at someone. I will tell you another story. I had a stage fright, though I had a lot of desire to be on the stage and speak to the audience so well that people get mesmerized by my talk. I always wanted to act and act so well that everyone should look for me in case of any acting requirement. Like most of you, I did not have the guts to go on the stage and face the audience. One thing I knew I can communicate well and both the languages English and Hindi and I am witty too. But then the stage was out of the question. I wanted someone to push me to the stage so that even if I do not perform well people will give me a bad name. They will think that I have been forced to do it. This is an act of cowardice and complex thoughts. But that never happened. In my first company, there was a cultural program that all employees and families attended. Anchor was fixed and various programs were planned. On the day of the program the anchor had some issues back home town and he had to live in that afternoon at any cost. He was not available for the program. Now who is going to do anchoring? This gentleman came running to my office at 10:00 a.m. and said he had to go home for some very urgent work and he was not available that evening for the program. Now look at his second sentence. He requested to do anchoring in the evening. Without giving a second thought I agreed with all confidence. He handed over the program schedule left for his hometown. I showed confidence but when he left I was in complete darkness. What to do now? Nothing was coming to my mind. I cannot even discuss it with anyone as everyone was fine with my taking over the show. No one know that I had never stood on this stage. Never done any program on the stage. After some time, I automatically got connected with my Sub conscious mind, which told me to go ahead and do the program. You have got command of your language and you can do it. Here I pulled my socks and wrote the program outline on my own. I went into the bathroom which was the quietest place in the office. I requested my housekeeping staff to put a cleaning board outside. I practiced for an hour. I knew I will mug up the first para to start the program and then I was sure I could conduct thereon. Since my language was good, the chances of getting fumbled up were very less. Now listen to all of you, the program went pretty well. Every year I started getting a chance to steer the program. I used to rehearse and practice a lot before going on the stage. Slowly I developed good confidence in myself and now I fearlessly go on the stage. But I rehearse well before going. I kept on becoming better every time as I kept raising the bar. I did a lot of homework and some research on stage fear and became better.

Last but not least, in the arena of self-development is taking training and coaching. This is the knowledge world you get many trainings and coaching online. You can keep developing yourself in order to improve. You do not have to go anywhere and can learn sitting at home unless and until you require a mentor for your holistic development. Portal like Coursera and Udemy where they train people on various topics. Pick up your area of improvement and get on the required courses. Therefore, there are three ways by which you can do sell development.

1. Throw yourself in the situation and learn.
2. Develop your own methodology of development. It could be observing or following someone.
3. Through proper training and coaching. Outline courses or mentorship programs.

Before everything you need to honestly identify the area of improvement which should be a holistic approach. Now find ways to improve or develop. You are the best person to know yourself. Please do not cheat yourself and do not depend on college or school to give you everything. Colleges and universities are dealing with thousands of students. It is not possible for them to identify individuals' weaknesses and prepare a related training intervention. It is also unwise to depend on colleges for everything. One should take care of one's personal development on their own. We are the best people to know ourselves. And we should take the onus of our own development.

ENTREPRENEURS' MINDSET

"Logic will get you from A to B. Imagination will take you everywhere."
– Albert Einstein

Everyone should have an entrepreneurial mindset while working in any organization and in any field. Entrepreneurs are always innovative and creative. They always think progressively and differently. They plan-do-check and are passionate about the work. Some of the qualities that every aspirant should bear in mind and take action accordingly.

1. **Take Ownership** - Take ownership of whatever you do or whatever you are asked to do. Once you are doing things, you should take full responsibility and accountability for the consequences. On the other hand, if you have accepted to do something means you have taken that responsibility and you should do it with full ownership. Now no looking back and start cribbing and blaming others for your decision. This act is an act of losers and cowards and I do not mind saying spineless.

2. **Set your goal** - Create a goal for you and be passionate about fulfilling the same. Keep reviewing to ascertain that you are on track. Entrepreneurs always make goals that will impact society at large. I am not suggesting anything to you guys but just trying to you're your attention about the thinking process of entrepreneurs.

3. **Be quality conscious** - Quality work is always appreciable. In case entrepreneurs have to be quality conscious if they want to survive in the cutthroat competition. I will request aspiring students who would become employees very soon should have this quality from the beginning so that the habit continues

4. **Brand power** - You are your brand. How would you make it more visible and lucrative in your call?

5. **Vision** - Have some vision in your life. I know in this nascent stage it is difficult but why cannot you start thinking? Are you enjoying what you are doing? Are you part of the herd? Do you feel close to some other work and start taking an interest in that more? The area that you have chosen for your career is yours or planned by your parents or friends. Keep thinking about these things, you will be able to get your vision. Initially, you will feel like a fool thinking about this and then later you will find the meaning coming out of it. You may get yourself checked with a career counsellor. These days there is software that can tell your liking and inclination for the work that you want to do as a future career

6. **Jump right in** - Do not think too much while initiating to do something, just get in and then start tweaking things to accomplish. If you keep thinking, you will never start and remain wherever you are standing you are. Here I do not mean that you become jealous of someone and want to take his place. It just means barge in and do not waste time and too much of thinking. The more you think the more you get an answer of not doing. Therefore, give some thought, believe in your gut, and take a call.

7. **Follow your passion** - Just do not give up your passion. Every passion may not fetch lots of money but look at the happiness and energy that it brings in you. You will start enjoying the work and you will be more than 100% of your ability. Your creativity will flow and you will never get bored. Quality of work will be far more than you can think. What is the best thing in your life which will keep you hearty and healthy? The answer is happiness. You will get immense happiness if you follow your passion. The tendency of students and their parents is that their ward has taken marketing as a subject, how can they move to HR? These are all unnecessary discussions. There are so many people in the world who took some line of studies for their career but later changed to some different career of their choice and are still very successful. Examples are Sushant Singh Rajput (actor) and the director of the film "Fukrey", Nitesh Tiwari. Both graduated from best of the engineering colleges. Do you know what are they doing now, (my heart is with Sushant Singh, a great budding actor, who enigmatically lost his life in June 2020 ... Om Shanti) There are many examples of this kind who has changed the line to follow his passion. Most of the cricketers fall into this bucket. Hence follow the passion relentlessly. Sit in the dark room with a glass of beer (even a hard

drink will do, a glass of rum, maybe) and give it a thought. Are you doing justice to your life and career?

8. **Do not let fear hold you back** - Remember that advertisement of the soft drink Dew" darr ke aage jeet hai"(there is always a win after the scary hardship)

   Though this is an advertisement but has lots of mettle in it. You will see all successful people have gone through this cycle. So do not worry take calculated dress and move on. Overcome fear or society's pressure follow your heart..

9. **Adapt to different situations** - With due respect to all future leaders, learn to adapt to different situations. This quality will help to reach high in your career. Your success should not get into your head, and failure should not ruin you. Balance your thought process. Every situation in your life is temporary, so do not get carried away or bogged down. Hold your breath, emotion, patience, and everything will fall in place. Be like oil which can change its shape with the shape of the container. It has no ego and adopts and adapts to the external situation as required. Therefore keeping prefixed thoughts can impact your adaptability and agility so be mobile. Accept it as it comes

10. **Get along with successful people** - Be in the environment of successful people. This will help you to get good vibes and thoughts. The level of discussions will always be valuable and useful. You will always learn from them which should always be your Motto. "Sangat se aadat " (Habit comes from the company you keep)philosophy should be there for each one of you. This will help you to stay positive with lots of good thoughts. Never hesitate to ask for help. Develop a good network. The network is the net worth

11. **Always learn new things** - Learning should be your continuous process. The day you stop learning, think that is your end of existence. In my case, I keep reading leadership and management books. I have set up a library in my home. I keep reading. This helps to increase my reading habits and learn new things. These days you find YouTube and other portals provide lots of learning. Just be in touch with any mode of learning but do not stop.

12. **Meet people** - Take out time to meet people. Invest time meeting people and your friends. Good friends are gold forever. They are the people who come to the forefront when the time comes. Attend seminars and be

physically present. Make your network, especially in this era of social media where people hardly meet in person. You all take my word and try and meet people in person.

13. **Make a first impression** - To sum u,p my submission is that all of you should think like an entrepreneur or owners of the company wherever you work. Your energy will start channelizing likewise and you will do wonders in your field, is my guarantee.

EMOTIONAL INTELLIGENCE

If your emotional abilities aren't in hand, if you don't have self-awareness if you are not able to manage your distressing emotions if you can't have empathy and have effective relationships, then no matter how smart you are, you are not going to get very far:

– Daniel Goleman

Over the period emotional Intelligence has gained its ground and is widely understood that IQ is important but if the person has good shades of EQ, then decisions made will be balanced and informed. Most of the decisions have the following things involved:

1. 1) How do you communicate the decision?
2. 2) What could be the impact on the person because of the decision?
3. 3) Society or any other section of people get impacted by the decision.

Many questions are to be suitably answered. Decision made by the person with more IQ was just the convey of the decision based on the situation without an iota of emotions. Though the decision may not be wrong the way it is communicated is not appreciated or welcomed. Even emotional intelligent would have taken the same decision but with different delivering parameters which was acceptable and appreciable as well. EQ helps in analyzing the situation before communication. EQ helps aspiring students to better analyze situations. It does not only help students to interact with each other better but also helps them to tackle academic issues with greater panache. The better the students take a grip on the situation, the better they can have control over it/them. This concept has been defined by Goleman who gave birth to the concept.

1. Self-awareness
2. Self-regulation
3. Internal motivation
4. Empathy
5. Social skills

Emotional intelligence tries to explain that regulates your thinking and channelize your thought process with empathy so that the decision or discussion will be acceptable / enjoyed by everyone around.

Let me give you a very good example from Ramayana on the E.I. When lord Rama was in exile, shabri gave him some fruits. She had already tasted all the fruits so that lord Rama did not have to eat sour fruits. Lord Rama understood the emotions behind it and ate the fruits she offered. Here the quality of Rama manifests his EI. Emotional intelligence is the ability to understand your own as well as other's feeling and how they affect behavior. An E.I. person is aware of the influence emotions have on people and acts accordingly leading to more successful relations all around. It is a very touchy moment though the outcome of the decision is the same whether taken by EQ or IQ mindset people. The difference over here is that EQ provides positive influence and is more impactful and acceptability is more across. EQ is informed action, Points below illustrate how to increase EQ

1. **Listen to others**-The tendency of people is to pounce in the conversation to share their thoughts without listing to others. This is damaging. Do not have any preconceived thoughts in your mind listen with both ears and understand the feeling behind it. In fa,ct help the other person with your value addition to the conversation.

2. **Positive attitude** - Make the atmosphere more congenial to enhance positive Vibes. Try and convert all conversations to a conducive one and develop relationships in the process.

3. **Take responsibility** - EI people take responsibility for their actions and do not get swayed by other person's reactions while blaming other person's actions for their reactions. They readily own up to their mistakes and focus on the main issue.

4. **Develop self-awareness**-Introspect and spend time with yourself in a quiet place to understand yourself better. It is obvious that a person who identifies with his emotions can easily relate to others' needs.

Aspiring students are our future leaders. In this era of 4.0 and 5.0 industrialization EQ has more roles to play in informed and conscious decision-making, bringing teams together, collaborating with others, and respecting others' views even if the person is his subordinate. The corporate world is changing in the VUCA (volatility, uncertainties, complexities, and ambiguity) world very swiftly and EI is the **buzzword** across. We all have to change ourselves with a pinch of salt to be effective in the workplace. The student should start adopting and enhancing these attributes from the beginning to be successful in the first employment from day one (beginning).

    * VUCA – Volatility, Uncertainties, Complexity, and ambiguity

CREATE YOUR OWN PROFILE

Every student must be wondering how to make his profile. There are many people/experts who will give their views. Hey guys I am not talking about your FB or Instagram profile which I know you all are experts in and do not need guidance. In fact, you all youngsters can become better guides for all of us. I will touch upon social media in the next chapter, let me talk about CV or Biodata. What do you consider while making your profile? You may pay money and take an expert's advice but guess what … you are the expert in this, with a bit of professional guidance which is free of cost from people like us, you would easily do it. Just think logically and go in the same way. Just think you are the recruiter and have gone for campus placement. What would you like to see in a CV when you come for a campus interview, close your eyes and start thinking.

1. Who is this person? So right your full name and phone number and email ID on top

2. What is your goal and objective –In two-three lines state your goals in objective. Also, write a couple of strengths that you have. 2-3 strengths are good enough.

    Now beware there could be competency-based questions based on your goals, objective and strength. Prepare them on a piece of paper for reference before the interview.

3. The projects or internship training that you have undergone, you should be good at answering questions from this project. Please prepare it properly. The best thing is to make a point-wise note and keep it for reference. From those, the project interviewers can come to your subject and connect the project with the subject. You should be prepared.

4. Mention any events, research papers, any committee that you are part of, or any social work that you have done. This work will reflect your leadership qualities and teamwork which is very important for any

student. It attracts the interviewer's attention. This shows the candidates' attitudes and leadership skills. You may expect some generic questions on this like the role that you have played. How many people were there in your team? Very basic questions just to know more about the events and your participation in it. If you have not done anything, please do not write. Never bluff and do not create a bad name for you. It is better to be blank than to bluff.

5.   Personal details – Last but not least your personal details like your father's name, where you belong, your passport number, date of birth, and your signature at the end

This is the chronological order you may like to follow as per my experience. I have visited more than 12 campuses and recruited more than 200 people from there, this is the more or less sequence being followed. Now you can do some very minimum beautification to look good. I am leaving it up to you to make it good looking and soothing. Do not waste time giving a gaudy and flamboyant look. Your profile should connect with your interview discussion. Therefore, you should know what have written. I hope you understand what I mean. Be natural in showcasing your profile. Do not overdo it to make it look too good. For the interview process in detail refer to Chapter 6 for the interview process.

SOCIAL MEDIA

First of all, let me submit I am not very good at social media therefore cannot suggest much. But with my experience, I can just add value that would be useful for you, in case anyone visits your page.

Do's

1. Make use of social media to showcase your creativity
2. You may write some articles and post your LinkedIn profile. Some events are pictures on Facebook.
3. Do whatever posting you want to do but that should either add value to you or someone else who reads it
4. Post some of your achievements.
5. Beware there are many students who are your competitor therefore be cautious in posting things on social media.

Don't

1. Don't make it a gossip site.
2. Do not post something which you are not and which does not add value anywhere or anyone
3. Do not keep putting posts because of some competition.
4. Cybercrime is very prevalent, so be careful. Put those data which cannot be misused
5. Be selective in following and do not get into an exchange of hot discussion.
6. No talk on religion, please
7. Do not disrespect anyone's personality or religion.

Having said that social media is the latest trend. It does not make sense that one will keep away from it. At the same time do not indulge too much in it, as it kills lots of constructive time which you can use somewhere else. Try to be wise and you know how much to be open and how much to keep in your folded sleeve.

TIME MANAGEMENT

"The secret of your future is hidden in your daily routine"
– Mike Murdock

Let me discuss this topic in the broader sense then I will come to the finer points. Though time management is a topic that everyone knows or is aware of either through their own consciousness or personal learning or training. It is in a true sense managing life. What is life? Life is nothing but time management. I am very good at time management, but not excellent. I like writing a "things to do list" in the morning either in the office or at home and following thereafter. Let me give you some examples to make all of us know how important time management is! All the examples which I am going to quote are told by the trainers of time management. My intent is just to tell you all that this is a very serious affair which is your life and does not take it likely make a part and parcel of your life. Thereafter it will become a normal routine. Secondly, I would like to give a context of my discussion to enable my content to flow seamlessly.

A. To realize the value of one year ask a student who failed his exam.

B. To realize the value of one month as the mother who gave birth to a premature baby.

C. To realize the value of one day ask for a daily wage labour

D To realize the value of 1 hour ask the lovers who are waiting to meet the partner. (I am sure this realization most of you guys must have experienced)

E. To realise the value of 1 minute ask a person who has missed his train.

F. To realise the value of 1 second ask a person who has just survived an accident.

E. To realize the value of 1 millisecond ask a person who has won the silver medal in the Olympic

There can be many examples to substantiate further but I am sure you all must be having many other examples of similar kinds in your life. I have just quoted a few to set the context. I remember an instance where we had to go to attend a funeral. We had to catch the flight to Bangalore. The flight was at 7:00 a.m. in the morning. We were eight of us who were going to attend the funeral. A day before I book an SUV vehicle. The taxi owner gave me the number of the driver who would come to pick us up. The month was November and the place was Delhi. November is a cold month. I spoke to the driver and everything was set to go. The driver was supposed to come at 5:00 a.m. at my place. From my place to the airport was half an hour. In the morning you expect the driver to come 15 to 20 minutes before the time to reach my house as agreed. The driver did not come till 5:50 a.m. I called him to see whether he has reached my gate, as I live on the 8th floor. The person did not pick up the call. I tried 4/5 times and the guy did not pick up the call. I have no option but to call the owner. The owner also tried to call the driver but again he did not pick up the call. The panic crept in us … what to do now, so early in the morning! The owner called another driver who took some time to come. By the time he came, the time was 5:40 am. and then by the time we reached the airport, the entry was closed. Just imagine my state of mind. I started shouting at the girl sitting at the counter at the airport. I was sweating in the winter season. I rushed and met the senior person on the flight. He said they cannot do anything now, but his next statement gave me so much solace you wouldn't imagine. He said he will accommodate us on the flight at 9:00 a.m. and there would be no extra cost. I was thrilled and then we traveled to our destination. My purpose in giving this example is that look at the panic, heartbeat, rough communication, and tension that you won't reach the destination in time and the very purpose of going was in vain the way I was sweating in the winter season and my behavior was completely erratic and anything could have been to me from a health perspective life could have been endangered. Though there was no mistake of mine but look at one and a half hours that I had spent till the person told me that he can accommodate us on the subsequent flight at no cost. It can happen to you also. Now the question is what is time management? Is it important for your life? Give it a thought...

Time management is nothing but helping one to achieve more in the time available.

The essence of time management is knowing what your values and goals are in your life and making optimum use of it to achieve these ends.

Time management secrets

TRADITIONAL	MODERN
Be quick to commit but slow to act	Be slow to commit but quick to act
Time centre approach	Commitment, willingness to do

Commitment is not the time you spend. It is the line you cross.

There are some standard ways to manage your time. One way is quite effective which everyone talks about but hardly people follow. And that is making things-to-do lists and religiously following the same. The things-to-do list should not only be restricted to office work. It must be your lifeline. The brain does not have the capacity to remember everything. There are so many things planned and unplanned, the brain has to bear and accommodate. It makes its own priority list in mind but again it has limitations and misses many important tasks.

2. Priorities your work by making and putting your work in the box below

	URGENT	NOT URGENT
IMPORTANT	Q 1 Urgent & Important DO	Q II Not Urgent but Important PLAN
NOT IMPORTANT	Q 111 Urgent but not important DELEGATE	Q IV Not Urgent and Not Important ELIMINATE OR POSTPONE

These are all standard practices but the best one according to me is making things to do list. As I said this is your life management, the most important thing of your life. Hence plan your life, set some lucrative goals, and do time management. All successful people are good time managers. This will help you to achieve goals and keep you healthy in your life. Health is your life, therefore, do a self-assessment.

How we spend time - evaluate

Learn to prioritize - plan

Act as per plans - implement

INTERVIEW IS A PROCESS

Does this need strategic Preparation? The answer is here

I understand some amount of luck plays its role in getting through any interview but this could be the case in anything that one does. Does that mean we should leave everything on luck? Preparing strategically for an interview is the only way to succeed. Therefore interview is a process and it is a serious affair that needs preparation.

I would like you to consider the following 3 Ps in preparing for the interview:
1. **Preparation**
2. **presentation**
3. **Preparedness: Accept the Outcome**

We can put these 3Ps into three baskets to explain the subject better. I have seen people missing out on these parameters and then leaving it on the luck to sail through.

1. Before Interview
2. During Interview
3. After Interview

1. BEFORE INTERVIEW –You should strategically prepare for it no matter how knowledgeable you are! Remember, the interview is a maximum of one hour and you have to sell yourself with your knowledge, presence of mind, and presentation skills. Let me further drill down:

A. Job Description (JD) – You should go through the job description (JD) properly and prepare accordingly This oozes confidence in you and chances of selection increase Make some notes if required so that you can skim over on the last day and be fully prepared.

B. Bio data - Go through it properly, line by line. You may have written briefly about your achievements in any past project, recall those, and put them in your thought process systematically. It is very important to read every line of your bio-data, especially some experiences of 15 years that you may not remember. Make some notes and be on top of everything.

C. Call for an interview - The moment you get an interview call, your interview process starts from that very moment. Let us discuss what preparation one should do for the interview.

▷ Gather Knowledge of the company - Dive into the website and get to know about the products or services the Organization is into. It's market spread. When did the establishment start? Who are there in the management? Look at the balance sheet, PAT, and EBIDTA to know the financial strengths of the Organization. This information will help you assimilate thoughts and impress the panelist.

▷ Remember the details of the past Organizations where you have worked. Recall some past achievements. You might have taken part in some forums or attended any overseas training, etc. Besides you should be prepared with an answer in case you have left any organization in a year's time or less than that. One has to be on top of the facts and figures and leave no stone unturned in your preparation.

▷ Freshers should brush up on their basics and be ready with some examples from the books. They should also remember the books they have referred to and the contemporary names of the books available in the market which will surely impress the interviewers. The panelist looks at your attitude, thought process,and knowledge on the subject. Divergent thinking will be appreciated.

Potential/hackneyed questions:

1. Where do you see yourself in the next 5 years?
2. Describe yourself or tell something about yourself.
3. Your strengths and weaknesses

Here interviewers check the quality of mind, communication skills, and forward-looking thoughts. These questions are too boring and hackneyed but one has to be prepared for these.

➢ **Date of interview** - You should reach the venue before the time for the interview. The candidate should be formally and soberly dressed. Meet the receptionist and inform your arrival for an interview and relax till they call you in. Your interview started the very time you met the receptionist. Just relax.

2. During the interview - Now you are called for an interview. Enter the room, stand in front of the interviewer, and say "good morning" in a clear tone while keeping eye contact with all of them. Positive body language emits confidence in you. Body language speaks more than your words. Say straight no in case you don't know the answer. Don't bluff! !. The first impression will take you a long and that could be the last impression as well.

3. After the interview - Get up and show gratitude towards the panelists, thank them for taking out time to interview you. Your body language should be perfect even if the interview has not gone well because this interview is not the end of the road. Then leave the room. Let me tell you even if you are not shortlisted, but have made a place in their heart that last long.

Technology in the Interviewing Process

With the advent of Technology, the internet, and computers have taken the front seat and control most of the business processes. The number of personal interviews has gone down drastically. People make use of Zoom,

Team meetings, skype, Webex, google meet, and other technology to conduct interviews. This has proved to be advantageous to both the Organizations and the candidates in the following ways:

1. Economical, Efficient, and Effective
2. Administration and Organization are easy and less time-consuming.
3. Process becomes faster and Quicker while TAT (Turnaround time) reduces
4. Candidates and Panellists can set the interview discussion from anywhere through video call.
5. More interviews can be conducted in less time and decisions will be quicker.

Today people do not have time. Technology is helping them to cope with the time.

Interview is a strategic process, if followed verbatim, the probability of success is more. This should be taken seriously and preparation should be accordingly done.

SELF-MASTERY

"The ideal Individual bears the accidents of life with dignity and grace, making the best of his circumstances, like a skillful general who marshals his limited forces with all the strategies of war… He is his own best friend, and takes delight in privacy, whereas the man of no virtue or ability is his own worst enemy, and is afraid of solitude."

– Aristotle, Nicomachean Ethics

Now let me try and sum up. Summing up all will mean self-mastery.

Self-mastery is the ability to control your own desires or impulses which means self-control and self-discipline. It helps you to recognize and understand your thought process, habits, and behaviors. It is the ability to take control of one's brain. My dear students you all are future leaders. All of you will enter the corporate world very soon. Today's corporate world is not like that of Tata and Birla where a person joins and finally retires from the place. They never think of hopping so frequently. They learn and unlearn whatever it is from those organizations. Do they have to grow their competencies? What are the competencies? Do they have to do anything more for the development apart from the good work that they are doing in their own area? Holistic views were missing a bit. In this VUCA world when uncertainty is hovering all around, the job market is facing tough times and with cut-throat competition. Therefore, just sticking to your own working regime and not upgrading yourself on a continuous basis is going to dupe down your career and your life too. Corporate looks at the overall and holistic approach in a person. These corporates have become so ambitious, and their requirements have become so complex that it is difficult to get the "all-in-one type" of candidate. What I am trying to point out is that be with the change and adapt quickly or you miss the bus. The job market has become too complex and demand for multi-skill candidates is increasing every day. Engineers are expected to have good communication skills, especially in English. Now technical people like HR and finance are required to know about the production process to a good extent. I underwent an interview, the guy asked three questions and I did not have any answers to offer

1.   What is an EBIDTA (find out) of your company?
2.   Which services consume the maximum money of the company?

Do you expect these questions in the interview where HR has no role to play? The outcome of that interview was that I was rejected though I learned a lesson and started paying attention to these bits. Now the hunt is that the person should be the jack of all and master in his own field. I would term it as complete self-mastery otherwise it is difficult. Therefore, changing yourself with the change is the only "mantra" to be successful. If you look from an organization's angle they are not wrong. Everyone should be knowing their production process and company financial figures. Then only they become true representatives of the organization. In fact, they look for other competencies apart from subject knowledge unless and until you are a fresher. They know if someone has worked for a couple of years in his domain he will definitely be an average person and know those bits. But his knowledge of other things plays a very important role which speaks about your competency level. Those people are termed as an asset to the organization. Why don't you start thinking and developing other areas and master that knowledge from the initial stage of your career itself and become an asset to the organization in the first year of joining?

You need to create power in yourself by going through step-wise / chapter-wise of the book and becoming a self-mentor. Some of the principles are

1.   **Obey yourself** - One who cannot obey himself shall be commanded by others. You can generate power in yourself by overcoming all the resistance. If we plan and cannot be disciplined enough to follow it till the end, then it is of no use. This means you are impulsive and emotional. If you cannot have control over yourself then someone from the outside end up commanding, you and making you work. Then you do not have an option but to follow. There are two mindset people created by nature which is on the basis of morality i.e. Slave morality and master morality. If you are a slave morality then you are commanded by others. You have doubts in yourself, and you will never have a real goal. Are you

one of them? I am sure you are not. You are the master of your life. You commit to yourself and you do without any supervision. I know you a are master of morality. You create your goals and follow and believe in acting independently from others in the pursuit of your dream. Obeying yourself is mandatory to achieve anything in life

2. **Strengthen your will** - The fewer emotional urges you have, the freer you are. For example urge for smoking and drink or waste time on social media. These are the time master. Avoid being slaves of your instant. You gain full control of your physical and emotional urges while strengthening your willpower. You cannot achieve self-mastery unless you have control over your urges of doing something which is not a good thing. Think that you have the power to really succeed and believe in that while keeping a positive thought process.

3. **Master your temper** - The growth of wisdom may be analyzed by the decline of ill temper. This means that by knowing how to control yourself, and your moods, you prove to be a wise man. I had an argument with a person. He shouted that me, and I did the same thing. He spoke some bad words, and I replied with the same, with worse bad words. What does this indicate? Your thought process is fully governed by the miss behaviour of the person. Where is your control over your emotions? You gave control to someone to regulate your behavior. This is utterly wrong. You need to review your thought process. You should know how to control yourself, your mood, etc. then only you will have self-mastery and prove to be a wise man. Otherwise, you are no better than an animal who cannot think and act on its own wisdom and thought by mastering your temper. Think before acting.

4. **Master your body** - There are two parts to your body number one physical part and spiritual part. Your body is your temple. It is your delicate machine that must be properly taken care of. A healthy body and healthy lifestyle lead to a healthy mind. Exercise regularly, have more sun and fresh air, and eat healthy food. Take care of your body's needs and nurture it properly. This will lead to a healthy mind. A healthy mind and body can be the best things that you can give to your life to be a self-master of your physical and mental requirements. They are properly taken care of every day

5. **Master your health** - Do not let your mind lose sight of better things and go for the wrong things which make you indiscipline and worthless.

Do not let your heart get broken and then you live life of a hostage. This means you do not have control over your mind and heart. Your self-mastery is endangered. Join in with good and reliable people who will respect, love, and encourage you to have confidence in yourself. Make a list of all the attributes your partner should have to fulfill your needs and desires. Mastering your heart means managing your love life and close friendship. It is perhaps the most important self-mastery. Emotional health impacts the mental health of a person and then everything changes likewise.

You need to experience things and learn self-mastery which is the overall improvement of your mind, heart, and body, all other things will fall in line properly once self-mastery is taken care of

EBITDA (Earning before interest, taxes, depreciation, and amortization)

CONCLUSION

Guys my sole intention in writing this book is to educate all aspiring aspirants especially the management and engineering students to see and develop other skills and competencies which are equally important. In fact, I will request the students to consider all the competencies and develop them wholesomely. I am sure this book is useful for everyone who prepares themselves for an interview. You cannot be satisfied with your functional knowledge, rather pay attention and get hold of other competencies also. You may get experience in this while working in your Organisation or you may like to obtain the knowledge from your own initiative. The fact remains that these are the requirements of the corporate world. If you want to be successful pay attention to all the required competencies and develop them. You may like to make some notes which will be a ready reference before going for an interview. This book will surely help you to brush up on your thought process and be prepared for half an hour to forty-five minutes interview.

These days' corporates are demanding, and they look forward to an individual having 2 to 3 competencies apart from the functional skills that they carry, otherwise chances of getting through become a challenge. Everyone wants to join the best of the industries, therefore listen to me carefully from this book. I have worked as an HR professional at the senior level (Now also I am working as Director -HR of an MNC) and have done many campus hirings. The **"B"** schools and Engineering colleges (**E** Schools) must tighten their belt more in this space to be successful. You guys have very peculiar feelings which don't work in this VUCA world where every industry looks for candidates who have a minimum of two to three competencies apart from subject knowledge. In addition, they look forward to new employees as **"Business partners"** and not as staff of the department. Therefore, the expectation is more from every candidate if one wants to fetch a job with better remuneration.

The feeling is that they have got into Management or Engineering Colleges, and now things will fall into their place as per the plan of colleges.

This thought is now primitive and does not work in the ever-changing economy. It is high time that all of you should start thinking of yourselves as business partners and work towards building the competencies befitting the Organisation.

Colleges are responsible for overall development. I agree to some extent, though not buying this thought completely. We elect the Prime Minister of India of our own choice. He will come out with some good schemes and regulations for the benefit of the people in the country. People of the country should take the maximum benefit out of those schemes. But do not expect Government to visit every home to see whether the person has taken benefits from the schemes or not. It is your responsibility (individual responsibility) responsibility also to ensure that you take the benefit of the scheme lest you do not want to reap the benefit from the scheme. But all these benefits are applicable to all of you. Another thought is that suppose I do not require that scheme because of my own personal reasons. Does that mean I will not do anything and wait for the new scheme of my own interest to be launched by the Government and then only I will consider, till that time I will wait keeping my hands over my lap? The enlightened answer is a big "No". We need to devise our ways and be on top of everything. Likewise, the colleges are doing whatever they could do. They cannot do a separate program for every student looking at the competencies and market requirements. Individuals should also take the onus of self-development. Think and grow with the college for your own future. This is part of the process of building a career. Your knowledge and upgrading yourself is not only useful to click interviews but it will also be useful in your career after you join any organisation. You will be the first choice of the management for any new project coming in because you are the readymade man for the organization. You just need a bit of brushing, and you are on the job and not like others whose preparation is not so good. You will stand out.

My dear students and other aspirants you should plan your career the moment you get into management or engineering colleges. Let me reiterate and re-emphasize. **You are the person who is solely responsible of the career.** Therefore, plan your future. The competition is cutthroat, you need to carve your way out. Jobs are available for competent people. You must attract organization with your skills and competencies. **Be a continuous learner for life. All of you are gems of the guys who need some chiselling through augmentation of skills and competencies**

TAKE AWAY

You should understand that interview is a process and following the process is the first step in landing a job for you, skills come later. Or by following the process skill improves. You must learn and understand the various stages of the interview from resume screening to finally getting the offer letter (**3 P process**). You should be fully acquainted with the process mentioned in the book. Prepare well and demonstrating your skills and competencies will increase your chances of success in securing the job you want.

The book revealed the match-making requirement of competencies in students and other aspirants either from engineering or management graduates/backgrounds. How do you improve your skills and competencies to become saleable in the ever-changing economy and market requirements?! Therefore, all of us should tighten our belts and plan our journey of success accordingly. From my experience, I can very bluntly say that pace up with the changing needs of the market. I would like to advise everyone (readers) to read the market requirement continuously and keep upgrading yourself with the pace and then you are limitless … Wow!!!. Hope this carries sense.

Let me give you a glimpse of some of the CEOs and VP / Director HR with whom I have personally interacted and requested them to give their thoughts on this they have the following things to say about employees either newcomers or already working:

1. They need to work like a business partner from day one while having a firm belief in transformation and do not spend their days in transactional activities, though later also has a significant role to play and one should not undermine. They should work like a business partner and believe in taking risks (though calculated)
2. They would look for candidates with good communication skills and a strong belief in working in a team, a good team player.

3. Employees focus should be on continuous learning and development for themselves and the team. Possess open-minded thought process while having a good vision for their own growth

4. They should be capable enough to connect their goals with Organisational goals. In other words, looking at the big picture

5. They need people with reasonably high competency levels apart from understanding their own subject.

6. They should keep updating themselves with the ever-changing market. This is a VUCA world and also a knowledge world, therefore they are required to be abreast with the latest happening in the market.

7. Finally they said that the person should be a good Human Being and courageous enough to call a spade a spade.

Let me put an end to my experience and thought process in this book. I am sure readers will get benefitted from it. It has references more to the Indian Context, but it's very useful and applicable to any aspirants who would like to crack an interview across the globe. Try and understand the intent and underlying meaning while following the process religiously and you will find the positive result.

Thank you. Appreciate your feedback if any on ramen4@yahoo.com with the subject title "the name of the book " which will help me to improve further

References:

I have referred some of the writers in Google Engine search. My own practical experiences while interviewing more than 1000 candidates of various levels including campus hiring. In addition to it my own readings from various articles and published papers